Table of contents

Kotlin_compact_ is for all Java professionals who want to get into Kotlin development with minimal time and effort.

In compact chapters, concentrating on the essentials, you'll get to know Kotlin within a few afternoons or some subway rides, and you'll soon be able to use it to write your own programs and apps.

As the title suggests, **Kotlin**_compact_ is not explicitly an all-encompassing work on Kotlin. Rather, I focus on the necessary foundations and best features Kotlin has to offer, and which I find to be most valuable when getting started with Kotlin development.

About the author

My name is Thorsten Schleinzer, I am a graduate in Media Information Technology and have been a professional software developer and architect for over 20 years.

For a long time I have been working intensively with different programming languages. I started with BASIC, got to C/C++ via Pascal/Delphi & Assembler and finally arrived at Java. Although I've been developing with Java since its version 1.2, I've been working with or am still using several other languages: C#, PHP, JavaScript/TypeScript, Ruby, Dart, Lua, Scala, and a few more.

But it was only with Kotlin that a new language was able to fully delight me and convince me of a change.

As **KotlinCoach** I offer comprehensive information, support and training for Kotlin: https://kotlin.coach.

Copyright

Quick facts about Kotlin

- In Kotlin `;` is not mandatory.
- Kotlin is *null-safe*.
- Kotlin offers 100% *Java interoperability*.
- Kotlin is *strongly typed*.
- Kotlin knows/needs *no primitives*.
- Kotlin classes have *properties*, not just simple fields.
- Kotlin offers *data classes*, with automatically generated `equals` / `hashCode` methods and more
- Kotlin knows only runtime exceptions, *no checked exceptions*.
- Kotlin has *no new*.
- Kotlin supports *operator overloading*.
- Kotlin functions support *default values for parameters*.
- In Kotlin, *function arguments can alternatively be referenced by name*.
- Kotlin offers *string interpolation*:
  ```
  println("Hello, $userName! You have ${inbox.size} new messages.")
  ```
- Kotlin distinguishes between *mutable and immutable collections*.
- Kotlin can be compiled not only to JVM bytecode, but also to *JavaScript*.
- Kotlin is fully *compatible with Java 6*, which is particularly interesting for Android developers, who also want to reach users who do not use the latest mobile devices.
- Kotlin is an *officially supported language for Android development*.
- Kotlin offers *coroutines* as an alternative to "blocking multithreading".
- Kotlin is *open source* and released under the Apache License 2.0.
- Kotlin is lead by *JetBrains*, the company behind "IntelliJ IDEA".

Understanding Kotlin code

Even as an experienced Java developer, it was not easy for me at first to read and understand the many Kotlin examples and existing Kotlin code - especially such code which made use of several of the many Kotlin features simultaneously.

But struggling understanding even short code examples of a new language - although you have been working with Java, for example, successfully for many years - is a major hurdle trying to familiarize yourself with a new syntax.

(Anyone who has ever tried to learn the touch typing system, although it has worked so well with only four fingers for years, knows what I mean ...)

In order to clear this hurdle as soon as possible, I would like to venture with you "the jump into the deep end" right away and carefully walk you through a Kotlin example. After that, I hope you will have all the tools under your belt not to be deterred by Kotlin (any longer), but rather enjoy a flying start.

Although it is relatively simple Kotlin code, even for Java connoisseurs it is not necessarily straightforward, especially because it uses and combines several Kotlin language constructs all at once:

```kotlin
val strings = listOf("Hello", "World", "!")
val lengths = strings.map { it.length }
```

But very soon you will understand exactly what this code does and - I am convinced - be thrilled, what Kotlin has to offer and does so much better than Java.

Declaring variables

Let's start with the very first line. It is a declaration of the variable `strings`, followed by its initialization.

Standing out right away is the `val` keyword, which does not (yet) exist in Java.

Also, the declaration of the variable's *type* seems to be missing. How is this even possible, given that Kotlin is a strongly typed language?

To get to the bottom of these questions, let's have a look at a similar example in Java:

Following is a declaration of the variable `i` of type `int` in Java, which is initialized directly with the value `42`:

```java
int i = 42;
```

In Kotlin, the same variable declaration looks like this:

```
var i : Int = 42
```

This looks a bit "reversed", compared to Java.

Variable declarations in Kotlin do *not* begin with the *type* of the variable, but always with the keyword `var` or `val` (the difference between these two will be explained shortly).

This is followed by the *name* of the variable.

Finally, to specify the *type*, it is immediately noted after a `:` . (By the way, the capital 'I' in `Int` is not a spelling mistake, it's because Kotlin does not know primitives - but more on that later.)

If you like, you can initialize the variable with an assignment just like in Java, as in the example.

var or val ?

What is the difference between declaring a variable with `var` or `val` ?

Basically it's the same as the one between

```
int i = 42;
```

and

```
final int i = 42;
```

in Java.

Variables that are declared with `var` (**var**iabel) can be assigned a different value later - for those with `val` (**val**ue) this is forbidden.

The same applies here as in Java: only the variable itself may be immutable. If the object referenced is mutable, it can be altered by appropriate methods/properties - no matter if `val` or `var` .

Type inference

If you look closely, you will notice that we did not specify its type when declaring `strings` in the original example. In most cases, this is not necessary. Rather, the Kotlin compiler can often recognize the type of a variable via the so-called *type inference*, if an initialization follows the declaration directly.

That's why it's enough to write

```
var i = 42
```

or

```
var map = HashMap<String, Collection<Long>>()
```

instead of Java's

```
HashMap<String, Collection<Long>> map = HashMap<>()
```

which only really became readable with the introduction of the *diamond operator* (`<>`) in Java 7.

In the example discussed in this chapter, the Kotlin compiler automatically determines that `strings` is of type `List<String>` . This is inferred from the return type of the standard function `listOf` , which is `List<T>` , where `T` is the type of each element.

Thus, thanks to the smart Kotlin compiler, one is usually spared from manual type specifications.

Of course, you can still do this, for example, to widen the type to `Collection<String>` , or simply because it meets the personal taste (or the project's style guide).

Speaking of `listOf` , even though I have not even mentioned this 'built-in' function, as a Java developer you can probably guess its signature - in Java, it would look something like this:

```
public static <T> List<T> listOf(T ... elements)
```

as a static method embedded in a utility class - let's call it `CollectionUtils` .

We could have imported it statically (not shown) to call it without the `CollectionUtils.` prefix.

In Kotlin, this is done quite similarly. But the signature is syntactically a bit different - and Kotlin even allows us to declare functions at the top level, without any class "surrounding" it!

Declaring functions

Spoiler alert: this is what the declaration of `listOf` in Kotlin really looks like:

```
public fun <T> listOf(vararg elements: T) : List<T>
```

Let's go through this step by step:

`public` is no surprise for Java professionals, so far so good.

Kotlin is lots of fun

But already the second keyword lets even experienced Java users down, because there is no `fun` in Java (well, at least not as much as in Kotlin ;-)).

Just like variable declarations initiated with their own keywords (`var` or `val`), functions are also declared with a specific keyword. Its name `fun` stands, unsurprisingly, for **function**.

The return type is last

As we have seen in variable declarations, their type is noted at the very end, after their name. This also applies to functions. Their return type follows the function name (and any parameters), separated by a `:`. So in our `listOf()` example it is `List<T>`.

But one after the other: following `fun` there is a generic type declaration `<T>` - exactly how it is done in Java.

The fact that the name of the function (`listOf`) is next, is likewise no deviation from the Java syntax.

But several of these follow within the parentheses:

If we omit `vararg` for a moment and look at the declaration of the (single) parameter `elements`, we notice the striking resemblance to a common variable declaration: first the name, then a `:`, followed by the type. Only `val` or `var` is missing - simply because in Kotlin function parameters are always implicitly `val`, hence "`final`". (This is one of the numerous opportunities that Kotlin uses to implement best practices which came up over the years and which Java has never been able to enforce due to backward compatibility.)

The `vararg` keyword is simply Kotlin's substitute for the `...` known from Java, which you would note down between the name and the type of the parameter.

As already said, all that follows is the return type of the function, separated by a `:`, and with that the function is fully declared.

Top-level functions

Do you remember that I mentioned you may declare functions without an outer class in Kotlin? So you can do without the "popular" utility classes like `CollectionUtils`, which are nothing more than containers for static methods.

`listOf` is just such a top-level function provided by the Kotlin standard library in the `kotlin.collections` package. So its fully qualified name is `kotlin.collections.listOf`. But thanks to *static imports*, which you already know from Java, you rarely need the fully qualified name, and just `listOf` is enough.

Of course, you can also declare functions on package level yourself and benefit from this feature.

Named parameters, default parameters & more

Functions in Kotlin offer many more useful features that you might know from other languages. For example, when calling a function, you can reference parameters by name or save a lot of method overloading by using default values for arguments.

But since we just started to get to know Kotlin, and further details would throw us off track at this point, I'd like to refer you to the further reading of this book for more information, or to the official documentation of Kotlin functions (» 1), if you want to know more right now. Everyone else, please follow me to the next line of the example:

```kotlin
val lengths = strings.map { it.length }
```

Higher-order functions

Now it gets really interesting, and Kotlin flexes its muscles.

If you look at the example, you will immediately notice the `val` keyword followed by a variable name. So we are basically dealing with a variable declaration, which is then defined by the `=` and the code that follows.

Now recall that `strings` is a list of `Strings`:

```kotlin
val strings = listOf("Hello", "World", "!")
```

Now we call a method called `map` on it - but that looks a bit strange for Java eyes. And you might think I mistyped curly braces for parentheses. But what looks like a typo turns out to be a very common and extremely elegant Kotlin idiom.

But to explain this, I have to introduce you to *higher-order functions* first, if you do not already know them from other languages. (I do not consider lambda expressions from Java 8 a fully adequate equivalent.)

> *A higher-order function is a function that returns and/or accepts other function(s) as arguments.*

This means that you can pass one function to another as an argument in Kotlin - and that is exactly what we do in our example.

The `map` method is part of `strings` (rather of its type `List<String>`) in Kotlin. (More specifically, this is a so-called *extension function* of the type `Iterable<T>` - such extension functions are another very clever concept in Kotlin - but to introduce them right here would be too distracting, so I ask you for your patience once again.)

So you can call `map` on `strings`.

If you have not already encountered it in Java 8+, you'll ask yourself, "What's `map` doing anyway?".

As the name suggests, the method maps or "transforms" one value to another. More specifically, calling `map` on a collection transforms each element in it, creating a new collection consisting of the same number of elements. Each of them, however, converted to a new value according to the rules of `map`.

Next question: "What does 'transformed' mean?". Good question!

That's exactly what we can determine with `map`. To do this, `map` accepts another function, which in turn takes *exactly one element of the list* (in our case, a `String`, since we call `map` on a list of `Strings`) as an argument, and returns "something else".

For example, we could write a simple transformation function that accepts a `String` and returns its length (`Int`).

That's easy, and with the knowledge from the previous sections, you may even be able to formulate it yourself, but certainly understand it:

```
fun getLengthOfString(str: String) : Int {
    return str.length
}
```

(The only stumbling block may be `length` instead of `length()`. Why this is will become clear in the chapter about properties.)

So far so good.

Now all we have to do is pass this function to `map`. `map` will then go through all the elements in `strings` and call our transformation function for each of them. To do this, it passes the element - that is, a `String` - to our function and accepts its return value, which is the passed `String`'s length - an `Int`.

But how exactly do we do that?

As Kotlin supports *higher-order functions*, functions (in most cases) can be treated the same way as ordinary variables. That is, for example, you can assign a function to a variable:

```
val getLengthOfString = fun(str: String) : Int {
    return str.length
}
```

Compared to a common function declaration you've already encountered, the syntax looks a bit different: The function itself is "anonymous" because we did not name it after `fun`. Instead, we declare a variable called `getLengthOfString`.

Which is of type *function*!

So now we have a *reference to a function* in `getLengthOfString` - that's something Java does not offer.

Once we have done that, we can pass that reference to `map` as an argument:

```
val lengths = strings.map(getLengthOfString)
```

This looks strange to Java developers, because `getLengthOfString` is not a simple variable, but a reference to a function. (In Java, a *functional interface* would probably be what comes closest to this.)

However, this is how we can pass `getLengthOfString` to the `map` function, which in turn transforms every element in our `strings` list, resulting in a new collection of `Ints` representing the length of each `String` in `strings`.

But what about the strange curly braces from the example?

To introduce those, we need to *inline* our transformation function:

Like any other variable, we can inline `getLengthOfString` by replacing that reference directly with its true value - in this case, the transformation function itself.

Sounds complicated? It really is not - and this is how it's done:

```
val lengths = strings.map(fun(str: String) : Int {
    return str.length
})
```

As you can see, we have literally replaced the reference `getLengthOfString` with its actual value.

But since the function is anonymous anyway and can no longer be referenced "from the outside", we can write it even shorter by using a *lambda expression*:

```
val lengths = strings.map({ str: String -> str.length })
```

These look very similar to those of Java: our lambda expression accepts a single argument `str` of type `String`, retrieves its `length` (in case of doubt please just think of the empty parentheses: `str.length()`) and returns that (`Int`).

As you can see, we have "forgotten" to explicitly specify the return type `Int`. And actually we don't need to: the Kotlin compiler infers the type automatically, because it recognizes that `str.length` returns an `Int` - hence so does the entire lambda expression.

But the compiler can do even more: although we do not explicitly tell it that the argument `str` is of type `String`, it does not get confused in any way and still recognizes that "automagically":

```
val lengths = strings.map({ str -> str.length })
```

But how does it do that? Well, the compiler knows that `strings` is of type `List<String>`. So the individual elements iterated over by `map` are of type `String` - so is the argument `str`. How this works in detail will become clear later in the section on *extension functions* - but at this time, we are still after the curly braces.

Fact is: we can omit the manual type declaration of `str`.

But we can take this another step further. If there only is *one single argument*, whose type is known, you can even omit its declaration altogether:

```
val lengths = strings.map({ it.length })
```

Ok, now the declaration is gone - but a suspicious `it` took its place!?

First, we omitted the type of `str` and just declared the name of the parameter to be able to reference it. Now that we even dropped the name, the Kotlin compiler steps into the breach and simply names the single parameter `it`, so that we can access it.

`it` is thus always the name of the one and only parameter, if you omit its declaration.

We are almost done and just need to get rid of those parentheses!

Again, the Kotlin compiler helps us: It allows us to note the *last* argument (in our case the one and only) *outside* the parentheses:

```
val lengths = strings.map() { it.length }
```

Frankly, yes, that looks a bit weird if you have a Java background. It appears to be a call to `map` with no arguments, followed by a misplaced code block.

But in reality it is the call of `map` with *exactly one argument* - namely the lambda Expression `{it.length}` - noted outside the parentheses, just like Kotlin allows.

It becomes more readable, if you know that there is a special rule if there is *exactly one* argument: in this case you can simply omit the parentheses.

This way, not only the parentheses disappear, but hopefully so does your possible confusion:

```
val lengths = strings.map { it.length }
```

Bingo!

We have reconstructed the call to `map` from the original example. It gets passed exactly one single argument, of type "a function that expects a `String` as an argument and returns an `Int`". `map` then iterates the `strings` list, calls the passed function on each element (`String`), adds the returned `Int` to a *new*, internal list, which is then finally assigned to `lengths`.

Phew!

As you can see, though unfamiliar at first, Kotlin's code is very legible and compact once you get behind the secrets of the many powerful and clever features that Kotlin's creators have built into their language.

Thus, now the "jump into the deep end" is done, and I hope Kotlin has become much easier to read for you now.

In the further course of the book a lot more highlights and special features of Kotlin await you.

Classes and objects

Classes in Kotlin offer many improvements over those in Java, resulting in more compact and better code.

Kotlin, like Java, is an object-oriented programming language (and has a remarkable number of functional programming features!).

So of course, it offers classes with encapsulation, inheritance, polymorphism and all other object-oriented paradigms, also known from Java.

The syntax, on the other hand, is a bit different, enabling you to write more compact, easier-to-read and, on the whole, simply better code.

A simple example class

```
class Person {
    val firstName = "Alex"
    val lastName = "Example"
}
```

As in Java, the declaration of a class starts with the keyword `class` followed by its name (`Person`).

Our example class `Person` has two fields - more precisely: *properties* (see later) - of type `String` named `firstName` and `lastName`.

`public` is the default

The first difference to Java is the visibility of those fields: While in Java those would be `package-private`, since nothing else is specified, the default in Kotlin is `public`, so that any properties and functions not declared otherwise are always publicly visible.

However, this class is extremely inflexible and thus meaningless: the two properties have fixed values that are assigned to them when creating an instance and, being immutable, they cannot be reassigned at all.

So the class needs a constructor:

Constructors

Unlike Java, Kotlin makes a distinction between the so-called *primary constructor* and any secondary ones.

The primary constructor of a class can be written very concisely by simply appending its arguments directly to the class name:

```
class Person(fn: String, ln: String) { // primary constructor
    val firstName = fn
    val lastName = ln
}
```

The parameters noted there (`fn` and `ln` in the example) can be accessed in the class body, so that the name of a person can now be specified individually when creating an instance.

Declaring properties directly in the constructor

For the common case of directly assigning constructor arguments to properties, Kotlin offers a very compact and useful alternative syntax:

```
class Person(val firstName: String, val lastName: String)
```

This does not only declare a primary constructor with two parameters, these two parameters are also declared directly to properties of the class - simply by the prefix `val` (or `var`). So this example is identical to the previous one.

The class has become so short and compact that even the entire class body including the `{}` can be omitted - it remains a correctly declared Kotlin class!

It might look somewhat more accustomed with a few line breaks added:

```
class Person (
    val firstName: String,
    val lastName: String
)
```

Data classes

We can go one step further by writing the keyword `data` before this (already very compact) class:

```
data class Person(val firstName: String, val lastName: String)
```

With this minimal addition, we have created a so-called *data class*. Such are extremely useful for classes whose primary task is that of a data container.

Data classes have a lot of useful features for that purpose. One, however, is a real relief for Java developers:

The Kotlin compiler *automatically* generates proper `equals()` and `hashCode()` methods!

To do this, it considers all the properties declared in the primary constructor, so that, for example, two instances of our `Person` data class are structurally equal if their `firstName` and `lastName` match.

As a further addition, a `toString()` method is also created, in the form
`Person(firstName = Alex, lastName = Example)`.

Another clever one is the `copy` method, which I will show you later in the book.

'init' blocks

Primary constructors are a great thing and make for the utmost concise code. Unfortunately, they have the disadvantage that they can not contain any further instructions except the implicit assignment of their arguments to properties.

To execute more complex code during initialization, one makes use of secondary constructors (see below) or so-called `init` blocks:

```kotlin
class Person(val firstName: String, val lastName: String) {
    init {
        log.info("Created new person!")
    }
}
```

These are executed during instantiation in the order in which they are declared in the class's body - so there may be more than one `init` block.

Secondary constructors

Like Java, Kotlin allows for more than one constructor for a class. These are called *secondary constructors*:

```kotlin
class Person(val firstName: String, val lastName: String) {
    constructor(firstName: String, lastName: String, parent: Person) : this
(firstName, lastName) {
        parent.children += this
    }
}
```

They are declared using the `constructor` keyword. If there is a primary constructor it must always be called. To do this, reference it with `this` and call it separated by a `:`.

In addition to the features described, Kotlin classes have much more to offer, and the already presented syntax has even more in store. In order to do justice to the title of this book, though, I leave it at this brief introduction, which is enough to understand the upcoming chapters.

Properties of classes

Classes in Kotlin have *properties*, rather than simple fields, with implicit and automatically generated getters and setters. Calling these getters and setters is no different than direct field access in Java.

A common source of superfluous boilerplate code (» 2) in Java are getters and setters for the fields of a class:

```java
public class Pet {
    private String name;
    private Person owner;

    public Pet(String name, Person owner) {
        this.name = name;
        this.owner = owner;
    }

    // from here on only boilerplate code
    public String getName() {
        return name;
    }

    public void setName(String name) {
        this.name = name;
    }

    public Person getOwner() {
        return owner;
    }

    public void setOwner(Person owner) {
        this.owner = owner;
    }
}
```

Of course you could just set the fields `name` and `owner` to `public` and get rid of the getters and setters. This would remove the boilerplate code, and also the access to the fields would be more elegant:

```kotlin
pet.name = "Tomcat";
// instead of
pet.setName("Tomcat");
```

While this would not be a problem in this example, especially for `name`, this could quickly become one with `owner` during the course of the project: imagine, not only the `Pet` should know its `owner`, but a `Person` should also manage a list of all its `pets`.

For this you would have to write a corresponding setter:

```java
public void setOwner(Person owner) {
    this.owner = owner;
    owner.pets.add(this);
}
```

That is done quickly. However, it is now more time-consuming and annoying to replace all direct accesses to `owner` with calls to the new setter. While all modern IDEs offer refactorings performing that fully automatically, there is a negative connotation due to the need to touch many source files for such a small change.

In order to avoid these situations in the first place and to take into account the obligatory encapsulation in object-oriented programming, it is common in Java to work with getters and setters and to live with the boilerplate code (or hide it with tools like Lombok), along with the renunciation of the elegant syntax of direct field access.

Kotlin can do it better

But Kotlin does away with this adversity.

The above `Pet` class might look like this in Kotlin:

```kotlin
class Pet(name: String, owner: Person) {
    var name : String = name
    var owner : Person = owner
}
```

or, with *constructor properties*, even shorter (but less suitable for our example):

```kotlin
class Pet(var name: string, var owner: person)
```

This already looks very similar to the version from the Java example, which dispenses with the getters and setters.

To change or query the name of a pet, this is enough:

```kotlin
val name = pet.name
// respectively
pet.name = "Tomcat"
```

This too is similar to the corresponding Java code.

Suppose again that a bidirectional association between `Pet` and `owner` should be established, so that our above setter becomes necessary again. This might look like this in Kotlin:

```
fun setOwner(owner: Person) {
    this.owner = owner
    owner.pets += this
}
```

But, unlike Java, we do not add it as a stand-alone method, but associate it directly with the corresponding `owner` field, or more precisely, the `owner` *property*:

```
class Pet(name: String, owner: Person) {
    var name : String = name
    var owner : Person = owner
        set (value) {
            field = value
            owner.pets += this
        }
}
```

The corresponding syntax is to note `set(value)` directly below the corresponding property, followed by the body of the setter.

Within that, you can use `field` to access the underlying field in order to assign it a new value, as in the example.

But we don't gain much with this syntax, do we?

That's right, because the actual advantage lies not in the *declaration* of the setter, but in its *call*: because that one *does not change*!

As before, the owner of a pet can be set by means of

```
pet.owner = Person("Alex Example")
```

and of course, the setter is still (implicitly) called!

Accesses to properties in Kotlin always look exactly the same, no matter if there is a direct and simple field access behind them or even a complex getter/setter.

This eliminates the need for later refactoring, and one can use the nicer syntax of direct field accesses over that of invoking getters and setters.

Even the notation of trivial getters and setters is completely eliminated, since the Kotlin compiler takes over: if you do not declare your own getters/setters for a property, the Kotlin compiler generates them automatically.

Java interoperability

You can use existing Java code from Kotlin and vice versa. A mix of Kotlin code, Java code and Java libraries in the same project is easily possible.

A very important feature of Kotlin is an extremely extensive interoperability with Java. Especially valuable is that in Kotlin you can continue to use just about any existing Java framework and Java libraries as usual.

So you do not have to go without slf4j, Guava, Apache Commons, Tomcat, Jetty and the countless other gems of the Java ecosystem!

Mixing possible

The Kotlin compiler can (simply put) handle both Kotlin code and existing Java code. Thus, it is easily possible to use both languages in the same project.

In particular, during your transition to Kotlin, and with a (large) existing Java codebase, it is a real plus that you are not forced to convert proven code. Rather, it makes sense to develop new components in Kotlin, while easily accessing your current Java code.

Of course, one can later convert existing Java code to Kotlin to take advantage of its many advantages. For this purpose there are tools/plugins that convert Java code into Kotlin code fully automatically. This works very well in most cases, although often less than ideal Kotlin code is generated and a little fine-tuning is advised.

Kotlin at runtime

Basically, the only difference at runtime on the JVM is that you need to include an additional .jar library (kotlin-stdlib.jar) - nothing else.

No semicolon necessary

In Kotlin, a `;` terminating a statement is not mandatory.

In contrast to Java and other languages, the Kotlin compiler usually recognizes the end of a statement even without an explicit `;` - for example by a line break.

The general rule in Kotlin is *not* to use semicolons.

Two (marginal) exceptions should be noted:

Multiple expressions in the same line

If you want to note several statements in a single line, they are separated with `;`.

```kotlin
val a = 42 ; println(a)
```

Semicolon after `enum` constants

If you want to add properties or functions to an enum class, you have to separate their constants with a `;` from the rest of the body:

```kotlin
enum class Weekdays {
    MONDAY, TUESDAY, WEDNESDAY, THURSDAY, FRIDAY, SATURDAY, SUNDAY;

    fun isWeekend() = this == SATURDAY || this == SUNDAY
}
```

No new necessary

In Kotlin the keyword new does not exist. New instances are created simply by calling a class's constructor whose call syntax does not differ from other member functions.

Consider this Java example:

```java
Person person = new Person("Alex", "Example");
```

in Kotlin:

```kotlin
val person = Person("Alex", "Example")
```

This is one of the many trivial things that Kotlin brings with it to save on Java code and get rid of unnecessary code.

No checked exceptions, runtime exceptions only

Kotlin only knows *runtime exceptions*, a `throws` declaration is neither necessary nor possible. Of course `try` / `catch` / `finally` blocks are available - just never required.

While Java differentiates between *runtime exceptions* and *checked exceptions*, in Kotlin there are only the former.

Checked exceptions

The difference to runtime exceptions is that any function that can potentially raise a checked exception must declare it with `throws` .

In addition, the client is forced to encapsulate the call in a `try/catch` block or to declare the exception's passing on with `throws` .

This is not necessary for runtime exceptions.

Therefore in Kotlin the declaration of possibly raised exceptions with `throws` is not necessary (and not even possible - the corresponding keyword is just missing).

Nevertheless, one can use `try/catch` - just like in Java - to handle possible exceptions.

No primitives (int, float, …)

Kotlin makes no difference between `int` / `Integer` , `float` / `Float` and so on - all these types only exist in their "object variant".

While in Java, especially when using collections, it is necessary to differentiate between primitives such as `int` and the associated object counterpart, such as `Integer` , this is not the case with Kotlin. Here there are (at language level) only the object variants, no primitives.

No performance loss

However, you do not have to worry too much about the alleged performance loss: whenever possible, the compiler internally uses the JVM's primitives to generate bytecode. In addition, classes such as `IntArray` offer special collections that are mapped directly to the JVM primitives.

Null safety

In Kotlin, the nullability of a variable is an integral part of its type. Fortunately, it is quickly determined with a simple `?`.

The infamous `NullPointerException` is probably the most common error message that Java programs produce at runtime. It is no coincidence that Tony Hoare, the "inventor" of the "zero reference", describes it as his "trillion-dollar mistake" (» 3).

While in Java annotations like `@NotNull` only slightly improve the control over the nullability of references, it is an integral part of the Kotlin language. There are real keywords and operators dealing with nullability, and the compiler also provides corresponding checks.

Declaring nullability

In fact, in Kotlin, for each declaration of a variable, one has to indicate whether or not it can ever become `null`. What initially sounds like cumbersome extra work, is in fact none at all. Kotlin makes it possible to specify the nullability of a variable very simply and briefly:

Appending a `?` to the type of a variable declares it as potentially `null` while omitting the `?` declares it as "never `null`" (@NotNull).

```kotlin
var nullable : String? = "Foo"
var notNullable : String = "Bar"

nullable = null // OK
notNullable = null // compile-time error (instead of a NullPointerException at
runtime)

val i = notNullable.length // OK
val j = nullable.length // compile-time error: nullable is/could be null at this
point

if (nullable != null) // check for null
{
    val k = nullable.length // OK! The compiler recognizes that nullable can not
be null at this point, due to the outer if
}
```

Safe calls

With the so-called *safe calls* Kotlin offers a very practical syntax in connection with possible `null` references:

```kotlin
val fn = person?.firstName
```

What looks like an ordinary access to the `firstName` property of the object referenced by `person` differs only in the inserted `?`.

This means that `person` may also be `null`. If this is actually the case, the access to `firstName` is suppressed (it would lead to a `NullPointerException` anyway). Rather, the entire expression yields `null`, which is then assigned to `fn` (which, consequently, is of type `String?`, by the way).

On the other hand, if `person` is *not* `null` the property `firstName` will be accessed and its value will be assigned to `fn`.

If one does not want to assign `null` to `fn` in case that `person` is `null`, but rather a different special value, there is also a syntax for this:

```
val fn = person?.firstName ?: "Unknown first name"
```

So you attach the `?:` operator to the safe call, followed by the value that it should return if the reference in question is `null`.

Of course, all this not only works when accessing properties, but also for function calls:

```
person?.saveToDatabase()
```

This will save the `person` to the database only if the reference is not `null`, otherwise nothing will happen at all - in particular no `NullPointerException` will be raised.

Equality and identity

While the `==` operator in Java compares references for *identity*, in Kotlin it is internally converted to a call of the `equals` method. The check for identity is possible with the new `===` operator (3x `=`).

One thing that probably most of us used to do wrong in the beginning is how to handle the `==` operator in Java.

Contradicting the intuition of many, it does *not* compare the *content* to which the compared references refer but their actual values (read: memory addresses).

Instead, in Java, the `equals` method is required to check the referenced content for equality.

Even if you've gotten used to it, Kotlin reminds you that using `==` for the structural comparison (`equals`) is actually cleaner and more sensible than just comparing the references.

Kotlin turns `==` into `equals`

So Kotlin internally converts `==` to the call of `equals` .

This means that in Kotlin you check instances with `==` for *structural equality* instead of identity, as in Java.

As a consequence, you will only rarely encounter the call of `equals` written out in Kotlin code, but rather the more intuitive and readable `==` operator.

If you want to check two references for identity, Kotlin offers the operator `===` (3x `=`), which does just that.

Default arguments

Kotlin allows you to provide function parameters with a default value, which is used if the corresponding argument is omitted on the call.

```kotlin
fun String.split(separator: Char = ',')
```

If you want to split a string with the above (extension) function, you can determine the separator yourself, but thanks to the default value , also omit it, if the , is actually what you need:

```kotlin
str.split('|') // splits str on |
str.split() // splits str on ,
```

Default parameters are particularly interesting in terms of class members, since with their help you can (often) do without the otherwise commonly used overloading of methods in Java. This leads to more compact, more readable code and less boilerplate.

Especially in combination with named arguments, default arguments are a powerful tool for more concise code.

Named arguments

In Kotlin, function arguments can not only be assigned to the corresponding parameters based on their order, but also by name.

While in Java you always have to specify function arguments in the correct order, Kotlin allows you to specify them in any order by referencing them by name.

```kotlin
fun createCustomer(firstName: String, lastName: String, receiveNewsletter:
Boolean) : Customer {
    // ...
}

createCustomer(lastName = "Example", firstName = "Alex", receiveNewsletter =
true)
```

The biggest advantage is the improved readability. Even without knowing the signature of `createCustomer`, it becomes intuitively accessible when called. Especially with boolean variables or "magic numbers" it is immediately clear what they do. So it is obvious that the generated customer should receive the newsletter, while in Java, there would only be a simple `true` whose meaning would only become clear by looking at the signature (or with the help of a modern IDE).

Named arguments are particularly useful in conjunction with default arguments.

A prominent example of this is Kotlin's `joinToString` function:

```kotlin
fun <T> Iterable <T>.joinToString(separator: CharSequence = ",", prefix:
CharSequence = "", postfix: CharSequence = "", limit: Int = -1, truncated:
CharSequence = "...", transform: (T) -> CharSequence = null) : String
```

Since every parameter has a meaningful default value here, you can specifically set only those parameters that differ from this default when calling:

```kotlin
strings.joinToString(prefix = "#", separator = ";")

// or, since the order of named parameters does not matter, equivalent:

strings.joinToString(separator = ";", prefix = "#")
```

This call joins the elements of `strings` separated by `;` (instead of `,`) and a prefix `#` (instead of none). All other parameters are set to their default values.

Kotlin offers many other clever applications combining named and default parameters. Likewise, the automatically generated `copy` function of data classes is constructed in such a way that you can simply create copies of an instance and only selectively assign new values to individual properties. Arguments that are not explicitly specified are simply copied from the source object:

```kotlin
data class Customer(val firstName: String, val lastName: String, val
receiveNewsletter: Boolean)

val john = Customer("John", "Doe", true)

// and his sister

val jane = john.copy(firstName="Jane")
```

String interpolation

Kotlin allows access to variables (and other expressions) directly from within string literals, usually eliminating the need for string concatenation.

Consider the following Java code:

```java
String name = "Alex";
String greeting = "Hello " + name + "!";
```

which becomes this in Kotlin:

```kotlin
val name = "Alex"
val greeting = "Hello $name!"
```

`$name` is replaced by the contents of the variable `name`, more precisely by a call to its `toString()` method.

The general syntax is `$variable`.

Please note in the example that the final `!` is automatically interpreted as *not* belonging to the variable name. This is because the Kotlin compiler interprets everything after the introductory `$` as a reference name until it encounters a character that is not part of a common identifier.

To resolve all the ambiguities, or to use more complex expressions, there is the alternative syntax `${expression}`, which is to enclose the expression in curly braces.

Thus, the following is also possible:

```kotlin
val person = Person(firstName = "Alex", lastName = "Example")
val greeting = "Hello ${person.firstName}!"
```

Extension functions

With the help of *extension functions* classes can be "extended", even if they are actually `final` - like `String`, for example.

Extension functions allow you to declare functions outside of a class, and yet their call looks like that of a *method* of that given class.

Example

Suppose that in a project it is often necessary to calculate the *square of an integer*.

A suitable function for this is a quick write:

```kotlin
fun squared(i: Int) : Int {
    return i * i
}
```

or, thanks to Kotlin's *expression bodies*, even shorter:

```kotlin
fun squared(i: int) = i * i
```

Since Kotlin allows functions on package level, you could easily use this function now - without any utility class.

But with Kotlin we can do even better!

Using a corresponding *extension function*, we can "teach" the `Int` class itself to compute and return the square of an integer.

This means that calling the `squared` method looks a lot more "object oriented", and the function "moves even closer to the subject":

```kotlin
val i = 42.squared()
```

With Java that would not be possible like that - and looks accordingly unfamiliar.

Let's take a look at the `squared` extension function that makes this possible:

```kotlin
fun Int.squared() = this * this // extension function

val i = 42.squared() // call the Extension Function

check(i == 42 * 42) // proof that everything works correctly
```

The declaration of the `squared` function actually looks quite usual - if it were not for the `Int.` in its name. Also, it suddenly does not take an integer for an argument anymore…?

Let's start with the unfamiliar prefix. This is called the *receiver type* and specifies the *type* we want to *extend* - `Int` in our case - followed by a `.`.

The function itself now lacks the argument `i`, so we can no longer calculate `i * i`. Instead, we use `this`. But how is this possible given the function is not even noted within a class's body?

Well, that's exactly what we have previously specified the *receiver type* (`Int`) for. It is the representative of a class that would otherwise surround the function.

So if we call the function - `val i = 42.squared()` - the instance to which we call it (`42`) becomes `this`, which is referenced within the function.

In fact, an extension function behaves very similar to one that is directly noted in a class itself - and looks almost exactly the same. There is one very important difference though:

Within an extension function you can not access `private` or `protected` properties of a class!

Thus, the essential difference between inheritance and extension remains: while inheritance is (hopefully) intended by the developer of the parent class, but at least considered, with extension functions you can safely extend any class - meaningfully limited to no wreak havoc.

Extension properties

Besides extension *functions* there also are extension *properties*.

So we can improve our example a little bit by declaring the following *extension property* instead of the *extension function*:

```
val Int.squared get() = this * this
```

Again, the declaration of the property differs from its "normal" counterpart only by the prefix of the receiver type.

Thus, the call is still a little bit nicer, since the empty parentheses are omitted:

```
val s = 42.squared
```

As with common properties and functions, it is largely a matter of taste (=style guide), whether one uses a function or property.

In that case, I would personally prefer the property - simply because I would consider the square of a number quite one of its properties, its calculation is not really expensive and - last but not least - the call seems more elegant without parentheses.

Summary

- Extension functions allow functions to be declared and called as if they were an integral part of the receiver type.
- To declare an extension function, precede its name with the name of the type you want to extend ("receiver type"), separated by a `.` character.
- To reference the actual instance of the receiver type, `this` is used.
- Extension functions are common functions in every other aspect - particularly they have no access to `protected` and `private` properties of the *receiver type*.

Scoping functions

On the one hand, scoping functions offer the possibility of meaningfully and expressively restricting the scope of variables and, on the other hand, of bundling associated code in a clear and legible manner, along with a compact notation.

Often times one writes code, which first creates a new object and shortly thereafter invokes some of its methods or sets some properties.

In Java, this might look like this:

```java
Person person = new Person();
person.setFirstName("Alex");
person.setLastName("Example");
person.setDateOfBirth(1984,3,5);
person.calculateAge();
```

Thanks to Kotlin's properties, you can write that more elegantly:

```kotlin
val person = Person()
person.firstName = "Alex"
person.lastName = "Example"
person.setDateOfBirth(1984,3,5)
person.calculateAge()
```

It gets even better with the first possible scoping function called `apply` (» 4):

```kotlin
val person = Person().apply {
    firstName = "Alex"
    lastName = "Example"
    setDateOfBirth (1984,3,5)
    calculateAge ()
}
```

And this is what the signature of `apply` looks like:

```kotlin
inline fun <T> T.apply(block: T.() -> Unit) : T
```

The function calls the passed `block` with `this` as its receiver and returns `this`.

So within the `block` you can access the calling object (the receiver) with `this`. And as usual, you can omit `this`, which makes the code so readable.

What makes `apply` even more versatile is the fact that it implicitly returns `this`.

This allows, as seen above, to create an object and fully prepare it in one call.

With `apply`, the creation, initialization and assignment of an object can be elegantly and compactly encapsulated in a single statement - resulting in very compact, structured and easy-to-read code.

`let`, `run` and `also`

In addition to `apply`, there are a few other similar functions that differ in how you access the calling object within the block and whether you return `this` (as with `apply`) or the result of the block.

`it` or `this`?

As described above, you can access the original object in `apply` by `this` (and can omit `this`, as usual, for better readability).

Besides `apply` there is an almost identical function called `also`, which differs only in that one does not access the original object by `this` but `it`:

```kotlin
val person = Person().also {
    it.firstName = "Alex"
    it.lastName = "Example"
    it.setDateOfBirth (1984,3,5)
    it.calculateAge ()
}
```

Incidentally, unlike `this`, `it` can't be left out, which lowers the readability. That's why `apply` usually is the preferred choice, unless your goal is to avoid <u>shadowing (» 5)</u>.

The return value

We got to know `apply` and `also`, which differ only in whether one accesses the calling object via `this` or `it`. Both return the receiver (`this` for `apply`, `it` for `also`).

But sometimes you just do not want to return the receiver, but something else. There are the counterparts `run` and `let` for that. They do not return the calling object, but rather what the called block returns. Just like `apply` and `also`, the only difference between `run` and `let` is whether the receiver is referenced by `this` or `it`.

The following table summarizes all this:

Function	Reference to caller	Return value
apply	this	caller (this)
also	it	caller (it)
run	this	block's return value
let	it	block's return value

Similar functions

In addition to the generic scoping functions mentioned above, there are a number of similar functions in Kotlin that are less generic but have a specific purpose.

The function `use`

`use` is the counterpart to Java's `try-with-resources` (» 6), which allows you to encapsulate `AutoClosables`, closing them "automatically" in a more readable way than ordinary `try-catch` blocks.

In the following example

- we refer to a file
- open a `Writer` on it
- encapsulate it with `use`
- use the `Writer` (`it`) to write a text to the file
- close the `Writer` properly

```kotlin
File("test_file").writer().use {
    it.write("Hello World!")
}
```

What stands out is that the last step - closing the `Writer` - does not even appear in the code explicitly. Because that's exactly what `use` does for us 'behind the scenes'.

if expression

In Kotlin, `if` is not just a statement (as in Java), but rather an expression, so it returns a value.

```kotlin
val oddOrEven = if (i % 2 == 0) "even" else "odd"
```

So `if` returns the value of the branch that matches the condition.

That's why the well-known `?:` operator in Java is superfluous, because you can map its functionality with `if … else`.

Incidentally, this also applies to many other expressions, such as `try` / `catch` blocks:

```kotlin
val contents = try {
        file.readText ()
    } catch (ex: Exception) {
        "File could not be loaded: $ex"
    }
```

Operator overloading

Kotlin supports overloading existing operators (like `+`, `-`, `+ =`, ...).

To do this, it introduces the `operator` keyword that makes possible overloads like this:

```
class Vector {
    // ...
    operator fun plus(vector: Vector) : Vector = Vector(this.x + vector.x,
this.y + vector.y, this.z + vector.z)
}
```

With `operator` we indicate that we want to overload one. This is followed by a syntactically ordinary function declaration. The name of the function indicates which one of the operators you want to overload (`plus`, `minus`, `div`, ...), which also determines the rest of the signature.

For example, if it is a unary operator such as `unaryMinus`, the function may not take any further arguments. For binary operators, there is exactly one argument - the "right-hand side".

The example above is the binary plus operator `+` which allows you to add two instances of the `Vector` class as follows:

```
val a = Vec(1,2,3)
val b = Vec(4,5,6)
val c = a + b // calling the overloaded plus operator
```

It takes exactly one argument, namely "the right-hand side", `b` in the example, while `a` maps to `this`. As a result, the function returns a new vector which corresponds to the addition of `this` and the vector passed.

Available operators

For a list of all overloadable operators and more information, see the official operator overloading documentation (>> 7).

Useful overloads

The Kotlin standard library also makes heavy use of operator overloading and provides (in conjunction with corresponding extension functions) a lot of "syntactic sugar".

For example, thanks to the overloaded `+=` operator, you can add new items to a list as follows:

```
stringList += "Hello World!"
// instead of
stringList.add("Hello World!")
```

I also like the following way to access the elements of a `map`:

```
map["Hello"] = "World!"
// or
val person = personsDatabase[42]
```

Kotlin has much more to offer

My goal with **Kotlin***compact* is to provide you with a *compact* and as easy as possible introduction to the development with Kotlin, reduced to the essentials.

Due to the wealth of Kotlin's great features and its active development, I had to omit quite a few details, or even leave out some things completely.

So unfortunately I've been unable to explain things like *coroutines*, *Android development*, *functional programming*, *DSLs*, *Java-Script compilation* and many more exciting topics.

If you want to know more about those, I recommend the following internet addresses:

https://kotlincompact.com
> On the homepage of this book you can find further, up-to-date information about Kotlin. And of course you can recommend this to your colleagues and friends, if you like what you read.

https://kotlinlang.org
> The official homepage of Kotlin is the definitive source of information and a good starting point to find many other resources on the topic.

https://kotlin.coach
> As KotlinCoach I offer training, consulting and support for Kotlin.

Now I wish you a lot of fun further exploring Kotlin with all its finesse, and sincerely hope I got you off to a good start with **Kotlin***compact* :-)

Thorsten Schleinzer

Appendix A: Links Index

ID URL

1 https://kotlinlang.org/docs/reference/functions.html

2 https://en.wikipedia.org/wiki/Boilerplate#Programming

3 https://en.wikipedia.org/wiki/Null_pointer#History

4 https://kotlinlang.org/api/latest/jvm/stdlib/kotlin/apply.html

5 https://en.wikipedia.org/wiki/Variable_shadowing

6 https://docs.oracle.com/javase/tutorial/essential/exceptions/tryResourceClose.html

7 https://kotlinlang.org/docs/reference/operator-overloading.html

www.ingramcontent.com/pod-product-compliance
Lightning Source LLC
Chambersburg PA
CBHW050935060326
40690CB00039B/528